W9-AHA-128

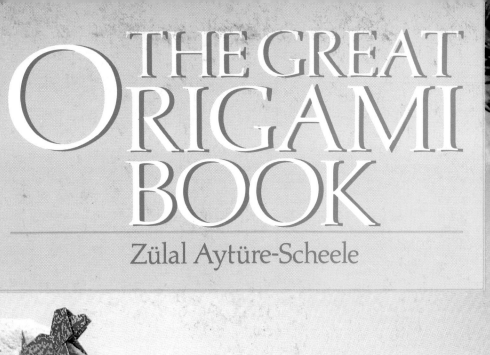

THE GREAT ORIGAMI BOOK

Zülal Aytüre-Scheele

Sterling Publishing Co., Inc.   New York

Contents

Translated by Elizabeth Reinersmann

Edited by Carol Palmer

Library of Congress Cataloging-in-Publication Data

Aytüre-Scheele, Zülal.
  The great origami book.

  Translation of: Neue zauberhafte Origami Ideen.
  Includes index.
  1. Origami. I. Title.
TT870.A9813 1987   736'.982   87-10062
ISBN 0-8069-6600-9
ISBN 0-8069-6640-8 (pbk.)

English translation Copyright © 1987 by
  Sterling Publishing Co., Inc.
387 Park Avenue South, New York, N.Y.
  10016
Original edition published under the title
  "Neue zauberhafte Origami Ideen"
© 1986 by Falken-Verlag GmbH, D6272
  Niedernhausen/TS., West Germany
Distributed in Canada by Sterling
  Publishing
% Canadian Manda Group, P.O. Box 920,
  Station U
Toronto, Ontario, Canada M8Z 5P9
Distributed in Great Britain and Europe by
  Cassell PLC
Artillery House, Artillery Row, London
  SW1P 1RT, England
Distributed in Australia by Capricorn Ltd.
  P.O. Box 665, Lane Cove, NSW 2066
Manufactured in the United States of
  America

Introduction

Even after hundreds of years Origami—the art of paperfolding—has remained an important tool in the Japanese educational process and is attracting new friends among young and old in many countries all over the world.

One reason might be that Origami as an art requires only a very modest investment—a piece of paper. Everyone who gets involved can create magical and beautiful figures and shapes. These small works of art delight the eyes, but they can also be practical, either as toys or utensils.

This book on Origami is intended to inspire and to stimulate.

Eight basic forms enable you to create 40 different figures. A piece of paper is all that is required and, on occasion a pair of scissors, or paint for decoration.

With some patience and care paper squares can be folded into perfect figures. It is a creative and joyful activity that is relaxing and gives a feeling of achievement.

Observant experimenters will—with a little experience—soon be able to invent figures of their own.

I wish you joy with Origami!

Zülal Aytüre-Scheele

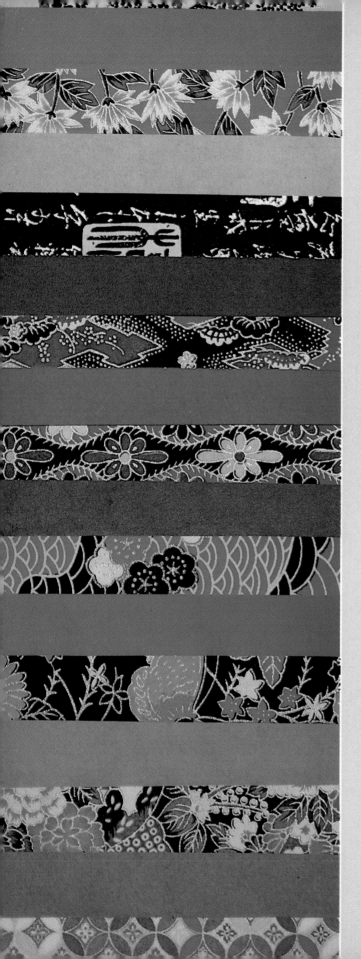

Paper for Origami

Since paper is the only material needed for Origami, choosing the paper is particularly important. Any paper that will withstand repeated folding without stretching such as giftwrap paper, writing paper, or paper from magazines is acceptable.

Experiment, and the right choice will be learned. The only requirements are that the paper can be cleanly folded and creased without tearing or ripping, and that it should have perfect right angles at the corners. So cut paper carefully and accurately.

Giftwrap paper is easily available, the choices are endless, and often the search for the right paper is just the beginning of the fun of the creative process.

Almost all of the figures in this book are made from giftwrap paper. Sometimes papers of different color or pattern have been glued together back-to-back so as to achieve interesting effects.

Of course real Origami paper can be purchased in stationery stores, pre-cut into squares. All figures, however, will turn out just as well if they are made with giftwrap paper.

The Ten Commandments of Origami

1. Choose suitable paper and cut to required form and size.

2. Fold paper cleanly and carefully, especially at the small points of corners.

3. Work on a hard surface, so that all folds and creases can be executed with exactness.

4. Exactness is achieved by moving thumbnail sharply along all folds and creases. All subsequent steps are then made easier.

5. The greater the exactness of a fold, the more beautiful the finished work.

6. Follow each step carefully in the sequence given.

7. Do NOT eliminate or skip a step. While folding, it is useful to remember the last completed step and think ahead to the one that follows.

8. Pay attention to all instructions, i.e. direction of folding, how a form is to be folded together, if it is a fold or crease to be opened up again, etc.

9. If Origami is new to you, get experience by practicing the basic forms. It is fun to discover how so many different figures are created out of a specific basic form.

10. To gain the most enjoyment from your effort follow all instructions and hints exactly and do your folds and creases carefully and cleanly.

BASIC FORM I

1. Starting shape: a square piece of paper.

2. Crease diagonally on dashed line.

3. Fold outer 2 corners so that they meet at the middle crease.

Hen

1. Begin with Basic Form I. Turn the form over.

2. At dashed line . . .

3. . . . fold left point so that it will meet the right point and, using dashed line . . .

4. . . . fold left point back to the left. Fold form in half at the middle crease so that the closed side of paper is on the outside.

5. Pull left point upwards and pinch to re-crease.

6. Crease sharply at dashed lines.

8

7. Holding with right hand, open form . . .

11. . . . fold upwards on crease 2.

15. Flatten form and press fold with thumbnail.

8. . . . pull left point down on crease 1.

12. Pre-fold on dashed lines 1 and 2.

16. Open point . . .

9. Press fold with thumbnail.

13. Open point . . .

17. . . . and fold on line 2 (see Step 12) to the left.

10. Open left portion and . . .

14. . . . fold down on dashed line 1.

18. Paint comb and beak red. Your hen is finished.

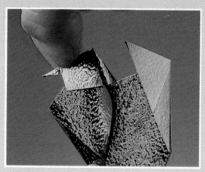

4. . . . take right point and fold towards the left, so that it will meet the first fold of the left point. Fold left point under on line 2 and out again on line 3.

8. Hold form, pull head slightly up so that beak is higher and press fold.

Duck

1. Make Basic Form I (page 8). Turn form over.

5. Fold form in half at the middle so that folded left point is on the outside.

9. Fold the lower portion on dashed line up to the outside.

2. Fold left point at dashed line 1 . . .

6. Head and tail are to be . . .

3. . . . to meet right point, and fold back on dashed line 2 . . .

7. . . . pulled upwards. Flatten form and press folds with thumbnail.

10. Repeat this step on other half. Fold corners to the inside at the dashed line on both sides.

11. This is your finished duck.

4. . . . crease sharply and then unfold.

8. . . . fold points back to the left.

Bird

1. Begin with Basic Form I (page 8). On dashed line . . .

5. Hold form on point A (shown in Step 4, center). Open form slightly from left side.

9. Fold form in half at the midline so folds are on the inside. On dashed line 1 cut "tail," on line 2 crease paper.

2. . . . fold left point back and fold upper and lower corners to the right . . .

6. Take left upper corner and fold to meet point A. Flatten down.

10. Unfold crease and refold downwards and to the inside. On dashed line . . .

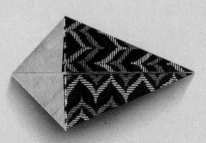

3. . . . so that they meet in front on the midline. On dashed lines . . .

7. Do likewise with lower corner. On dashed lines . . .

11. . . . fold "wing" upwards, ditto for the opposite side. Your bird is finished—ready to fly!

7. . . . while pulling the right corner upwards. Flatten form and press with thumbnail.

Parrot

1. Begin with Step 8 of Bird (page 12). Turn form over, and . . .

4. . . . fold the upper and lower cut edges of the small rectangles towards the middle.

8. On dashed lines 1 and 2 make sharp creases. Open the "tail" and fold inward on crease 1 . . .

2. . . . cut along dashed lines at the upper and lower edge of the rectangle approximately to the middle.

5. Fold form together at center. Make a sharp crease at the dashed line.

9. . . . then pull tail up and fold outward on crease 2 so that it covers crease 1.

3. At the dashed lines . . .

6. Open left corner and fold inward at the crease . . .

10. All your parrot has to do now is learn how to talk.

13

4. Repeat with lower corner.

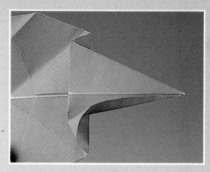

9. . . . fold up; flatten the resulting small triangle down.

Leaf

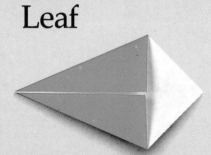

1. Begin with Basic Form I (page 8). Fold upper and lower right edges . . .

5. Fold form in half with folds inside. At midline and along dashed lines . . .

6. . . . crease in the manner shown in Hen, Steps 6–11 (pages 8 and 9).

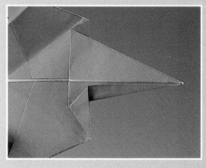

10. Repeat on upper portion.

2. . . . towards horizontal midline. Crease the upper and lower corners on dashed lines.

7. Open midline crease so that form is open as in Step 4. On dashed line 1 fold to the left and on line 2 fold . . .

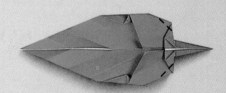

11. Crease upper and lower corners on dashed lines.

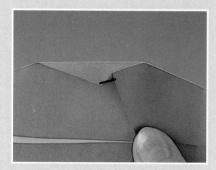

3. Open crease and turn point inward and press fold down.

8. . . . to the right. Press folds down with thumbnail. On dashed line . . .

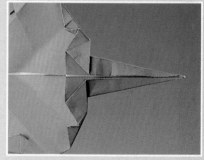

12. Turn folds to the inside. Press down. If you turn the form around you have a leaf.

BASIC FORM II

3. Fold upper and lower edges to meet on horizontal midline and unfold again.

6. Lift lower edges and pull up and out . . .

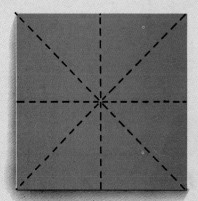

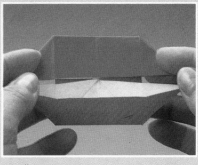

1. Crease a square piece of paper on dashed lines.

4. On dashed lines . . .

7. . . . and fold to meet horizontal midline.

2. Fold left and right edges to meet on vertical midline. White side of paper is inside.

5. . . . crease, by folding left corner right and right corner left.

8. Repeat Steps 6 and 7 with the top.

9. This is Basic Form II.

15

Sailboat

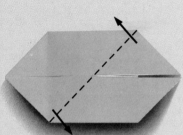

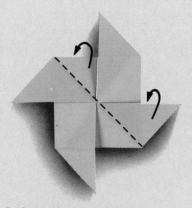

1. Start with Basic Form II (page 15). On dashed line fold upper right point up at the top half of the diagonal line . . .

3. On dashed line fold form together diagonally, folded side of form to the outside.

5. Pull right lower point to the right.

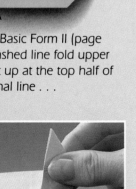

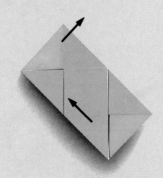

2. . . . and lower left point down at the bottom half of the diagonal line.

4. Fold upper left point up and lower right point to the left.

6. This is your sailboat.

House

1. Begin at Step 3 of Basic Form II (page 15). On dashed lines fold upper flap . . .

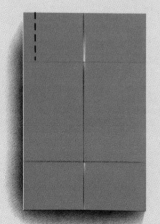

2. . . . up, and lower flap down. On dashed line . . .

3. . . . fold upper left edge to the right. Press the resulting small triangle . . .

4. . . . down and flatten.

5. Repeat on the other three corners of the form.

6. Fold form together on midline. Crease corners along dashed lines.

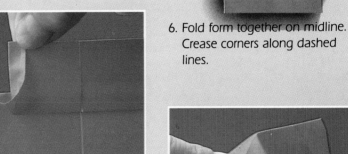

7. Open form slightly and fold top left and right points in.

8. Paint or glue door and windows on to finish the house.

17

Pig

1. Begin with Basic Form II (page 15) after Step 2.

2. Fold form in half at midline so folds are outside with foldline at bottom. On dashed lines . . .

3. . . . fold front upper and lower points down to meet lower edge. Repeat with back corners, folding to the back.

4. Fold right front flap up. Pull upper right point down . . .

5. . . . towards lower edge.

6. Flatten form.

7. Repeat on upper left side. Turn form over and repeat procedure. On dashed line fold inner left corner down to meet vertical crease line.

8. Repeat for left inner corner at back (will be the right-hand side when flipped over). At dashed line . . .

18

9. . . . crease right point to the left.

13. Press form together again. On dashed line . . .

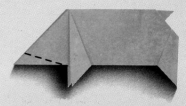

17. Press form together. Crease on dashed line.

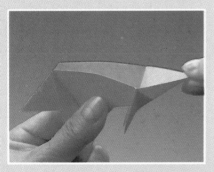

10. Return right point to original position, open form slightly from the top. . .

14. . . . fold point in. Repeat on other side.

18. Open form slightly . . .

11. . . . and fold right point in . . .

15. Open form slightly again at the top. Take the large point folded in at Step 12. . .

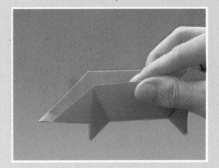

19. . . . take left point and fold up in crease.

12. . . . at crease created by Step 9.

16. . . . crease, fold to the right, and pull partially out to create a little tail.

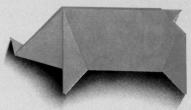

20. Open form slightly to stand it up.

BASIC FORM III

1. Begin with a square piece of paper.

2. Fold diagonally (white side of paper inside).

3. Fold left and right corners down on dashed lines.

4. This is Basic Form III.

Fly

1. Begin with Basic Form III, the open portion up. On dashed lines. . .

2. . . . fold both top points down. On dashed line . . .

3. . . . fold front top-point down and on dashed line (horizontal midline) . . .

4. . . . fold down again. On dashed lines . . .

5. . . . fold left and right corners to the back. On dashed lines . . .

6. . . . fold top point back. On dashed lines fold left and right upper corners forward.

20

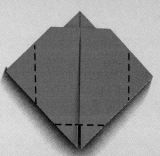

5. Crease sharply on dashed lines.

6. Open left side slightly. Fold bottom of point inside to form wing.

7. Open left side slightly and press leftmost corner in.

Ladybug

3. . . . down and the lower (top) corner up. On dashed line . . .

1. Start with Basic Form III (page 20), open portion pointing down. Turn form over.

2. On dashed lines fold upper corner . . .

4. . . . fold upper corner up again. Turn form over.

8. Repeat Steps 6 and 7 on right side. Glue or paint dots on wings, paint head black.

BASIC FORM IV

Salt-and-Pepper Dish

1. A square piece of paper is creased twice and the four corners . . .

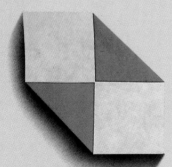

2. . . . are folded towards the middle.

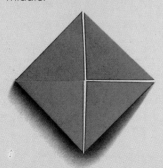

3. This is Basic Form IV.

1. Start with Basic Form IV. Turn form over.

2. Fold all four corners again to meet at the middle.

3. Crease on dashed lines.

4. Fold form together so triangle shapes are on inside, square shapes on outside.

5. Reach into pockets with four fingers and press form together in the middle.

6. Turn form over. Fill with salt and pepper.

22

For a game of chance, paint the inside in two different colors.

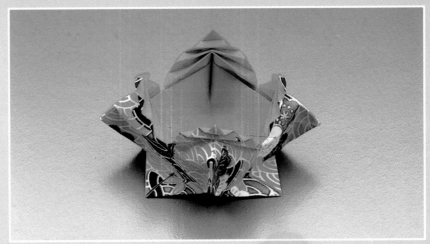

The form can be snapped open to either of the two views shown. You can play a guessing game with someone . . .

. . . or use the form as a finger puppet. Tape opposite adjacent corners on the inside, as shown, and draw a face on.

Spanish Box

1. Begin with Step 3 of the salt-and-pepper dish. Turn over. Take the four triangles meeting in the middle . . .

2. . . . and fold them out along dashed lines so points meet the outside edges. Turn form over.

3. Crease the four squares on dashed lines as shown . . .

4. . . . and fold in accordion fashion.

5. Press each corner together on the edges until the inside forms a square.

Box

7. By opening form at the midline . . .

1. Start with Basic Form IV (page 22). Fold all four corners to the inside along dashed lines.

4. . . . so that they meet at the midline. Fold upper "wing" at left center to the right so that it resembles photo on right. Fold small triangles in on dashed lines.

8. . . . you have a nest for the baby bird (page 74).

2. Each corner will now meet the midpoint of the inside edge. Turn form over.

5. Fold center wing back to the left.

9. Crease the form on dashed lines and open at the midline to make a box.

3. Fold left and right edges on dashed lines . . .

6. Repeat steps 4–6 on right side.

10. To make the lid, take a piece of paper that is approximately 1/16 of an inch (0.5 cm) larger than the one used for the bottom and repeat the procedure.

BASIC FORM V

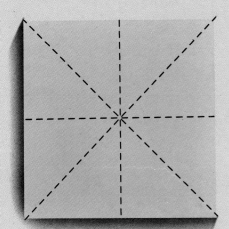

1. Crease a square piece of paper along the dashed lines . . .

2. . . . in order to create the necessary creases.

3. Fold paper in half (white side inside).

4. With fold at top, pull up right side . . .

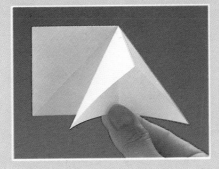

5. . . . fold open . . .

6. . . . push down in the middle . . .

7. . . . press triangle down . . .

8. . . . fold left portion of triangle to the right.

9. Turn over and repeat Steps 4–8 with the left portion of form.

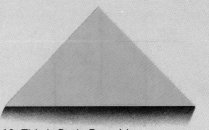

10. This is Basic Form V.

25

Barn

1. Start with Basic Form V (page 25). Fold corners up on dashed lines . . .

4. Lift right triangular portion up.

8. Open right half at inner corner and pull to the right while flattening upper portion into a triangle.

2. . . . to meet upper corner. Turn form over.

5. Open fold and flatten, creating a square shape.

9. Repeat procedure on left side. On dashed line . . .

3. Repeat Steps 1 and 2. Crease on dashed line.

6. Repeat Steps 4 and 5 with left triangular portion. Turn form over and repeat procedure. Crease on dashed lines . . .

10. . . . the small triangle in the middle of the house is folded up. This is your barn.

Eagle

4. Turn form over and repeat Steps 2 and 3. Fold both lower edges of the top form up so that they meet at the midline.

8. . . . and fold both corners down to midline. Turn form over.

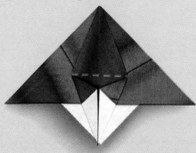

1. Start with Basic Form V (page 25). Crease on dashed line.

5. Crease dashed line by pulling lower point of top form up to the top point . . .

9. On dashed lines fold left and right edge of top form . . .

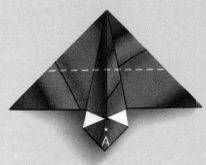

2. Pull up right upper portion.

6. . . . bring down again and unfold Step 5. Open this form slowly . . .

10. . . . to meet at midline. On dashed line . . .

3. Open and flatten fold into a shape whose midline meets the midline underneath.

7. . . . pull lower point up to top point . . .

11. . . . fold upper point down to A and pull B and C . . .

12. . . . together on midline, and . . .

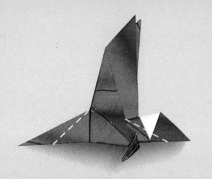

16. Crease on dashed lines . . .

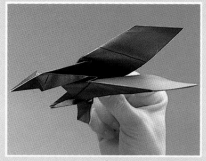

20. . . . first bend left point up on fold 1 and . . .

13. . . . flatten folds on upper edge.

17. . . . open left point . . .

21. . . . down on fold 2. Now pull point down a little more.

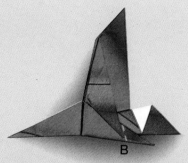

14. Fold in half, folds to the outside. Crease on dashed line at B . . .

18. . . . and bend down on crease.

22. Crease on dashed line . . .

15. . . . and fold point down.

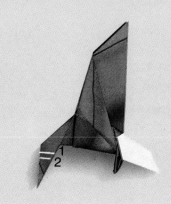

19. Repeat with right portion. On dashed lines . . .

23. . . . open point down slightly and bend down. Your eagle is ready to take wing.

BASIC FORM VI

3. Pull up right half of triangle . . .

6. Fold left half of the diamond . . .

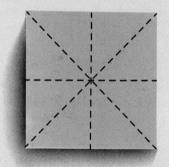

1. Crease a square piece of paper on dashed lines: press with thumbnail along each crease to get sharp creases.

4. . . . open, and . . .

7. . . . to the right.

8. Repeat Steps 3–7 on left half of triangle.

2. Fold diagonally.

5. . . . flatten down the diamond shape.

9. This is Basic Form VI.

7. You will have four wings on each side of the form.

Blossom

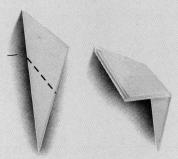

1. Begin with Basic Form VI (page 30). Open corners point up. On dashed lines . . .

4. . . . into a small triangle, whose left half . . .

8. Fold form together on midline and bend over on dashed line. Open up upper part of the form and pull down . . .

2. . . . lift right wing up . . .

5. . . . is folded to the right.

9. . . . on top points. Press blossom petals together in the middle from the outside.

3. . . . open and flatten . . .

6. Repeat all steps with the left wing. Turn form over and repeat all steps.

10. Tie blossoms to a twig or branch that has tiny green leaves (top left photo).

31

Canterbury Bells

6. Fold front top point down to lower point. Crease on dashed lines.

You need two pieces of paper of equal size but contrasting colors: A and B.

A: Outer Petals

1. Fold paper according to Basic Form VI (page 30), open corners pointing up. On dashed lines . . .

2. . . . fold left and right corners to meet center point.

3. Turn form over, repeat previous steps and unfold all folds.

4. Open form slightly and fold corner inside and flatten form.

5. Repeat Step 4 on the rest of the corners.

7. Open left half in the middle . . .

8. . . . and fold top point left until vertical midline is horizontal, halfway down. Press.

9. Repeat with right half.

32

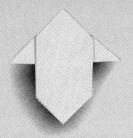

10. Fold lower point back up.

11. Fold left half to the right: left-hand triangle will be pulled up by this action. Repeat on right half. From original position with two wings on each side . . .

12. . . . turn top right wing to the left, bottom left wing underneath to the right. Repeat Steps 6–10. Cut lower point on dashed line.

13. This is the outer part of your Canterbury Bell.

B: Inner Petals

1. Fold paper B like paper A up to and including Step 6.

2. Push form B with open points into form A.

3. The four small points of form A correspond to those of form B.

4. For a stem wrap green crêpe paper around soft wire.

Cloverleaf

1. Starting point is Step 3 of form A (Canterbury Bells). Fold right and left lower edge . . .

2. . . . of front portion to meet the midline. Turn form over and repeat procedure. Cut on dashed line 1. Crease on dashed line 2.

3. Open and crease top portion and your cloverleaf is finished.

Leaf:

1. Fold a square piece of paper along lines . . .

Pansy

Blossom:

1. Begin with Basic Form VI— Step 7 of Blossom (page 31). On dashed line . . .

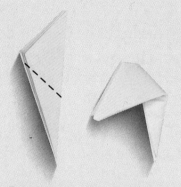

3. Fold form together at midline. Crease on dashed line.

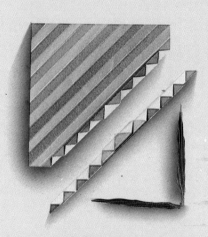

2. . . . in accordion fashion. Fold form together in the middle . . .

2. . . . fold top point of first "wing" inside.

4. Open top portion of form and fold the remaining three triangles out. Crease tips outward.

3. . . . hold there, and open both halves.

Snail

The paper used for this figure should be thin and the edges of the square should be 6 inches (15 cm) in length.

1. Begin with Step 7, Blossom (page 31).

3. Open top point of first wing . . .

5. On dashed line . . .

2. Fold upper short edges to meet on midline. Crease on dashed line, open previous folds again.

4. . . . and pull down to lower point. At the same time press left and right corners to meet midline. Flatten folds.

6. . . . fold lower portion up. On dashed line . . .

35

7. . . . fold same portion down again. On dashed line fold left and right edge of triangle . . .

10. . . . to the left. On dashed lines . . .

13. . . . to the left. Fold big right wing . . .

8. . . . to meet on midline. Press small triangular shapes down.

11. . . . fold right upper edge of top wing three times to the left . . .

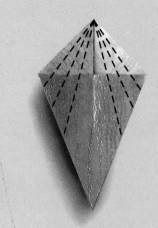

14. . . . to the left also. Fold the top left and the two right edges along dashed lines . . .

9. Fold lower right wing . . .

12. . . . so that the edge created will meet exactly on the midline. Fold the small wing that was created . . .

15. . . . three times (see Step 11). New edge thereby created will meet on midline. The top four wings of the left half . . .

16. . . . are to be folded to the right.

19. . . . fold right point left, and left point right. On new dashed lines . . .

22. Crease along horizontal line, fold left and right corners back on dashed lines.

17. Repeat Steps 10–15 on left half of the form, reversing all directions. The wings on the right side . . .

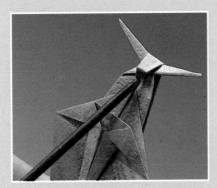

20. . . . fold top point over, down, and underneath the "feeler." This is the head of the snail.

23. Push bottom point against horizontal crease and carefully pull open all folds . . .

18. . . . are to be folded to the left as shown. On dashed lines . . .

21. Turn form over.

24. . . . thereby rounding out the snail's shell.

Cap

1. Start with Basic Form VI (page 30), open portion pointing down. On dashed lines . . .

2. . . . fold edges of top portion, one over the other.

3. Open these folds again, lift the left portion of the left wing . . .

4. . . . straight up, open fold and flatten.

5. Now lift right portion up and do likewise. On dashed line 1 fold . . .

6. . . . point of triangle down and on dashed line 2 fold under.

7. Turn form over. Repeat Steps 2–6.

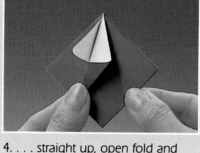

8. Pull both top points apart, open form.

9. Fold either one of the points down on dashed lines until it is even with the side edge of the form.

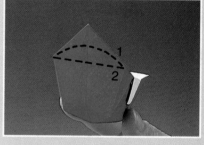

10. Cut the other point along dashed line 1 and fold out on dashed line 2.

11. Shape cap.

3. . . . fold top point down.

4. Unfold last three folds.

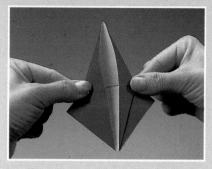

7. Press left and right corner so that the edges meet on the midline and form a diamond.

8. Press down fold. Turn form over. Repeat Steps 2–7.

BASIC FORM VII

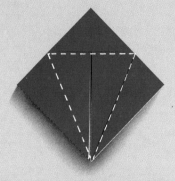

1. Begin with Basic Form VI on page 30, open corners pointing down. On dashed lines . . .

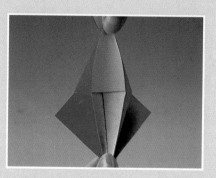

5. Open up top wing at bottom point . . .

2. . . . fold right and left lower edge of top wing towards midline. On horizontal dashed line . . .

6. . . . and pull upwards as far as possible.

9. This is Basic Form VII.

Horse

7. Fold form in half so that the portion just folded down remains outside.

Front:

1. Start with Basic Form VII (page 40), with the "split" side with two side-by-side triangles pointing down. Crease on dashed lines.

4. Open form; at crease 1 fold outer edges up so triangle is halved, and fold inside at crease 2.

8. This is the head of the horse: pull it upwards and crease in place. Crease on dashed line . . .

2. Open left portion of form and fold up and in.

5. Repeat on right side. On dashed lines . . .

9. . . . open top point and fold at the crease inside to the right: this is the mane.

3. Repeat on right side. Crease on dashed line 1 through the middle, and on dashed line 2.

6. . . . fold front top point down twice.

10. Fold both corners of the mane down and forward. On dashed line . . .

41

11. . . . open lower right portion and fold downwards and inward on crease.

12. Crease on dashed line . . .

13. . . . open the lower portion and fold towards right on crease.

14. Repeat with left side.

Back:

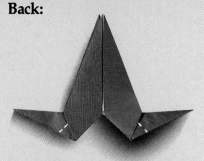

1. Fold second piece of paper up to Step 2 of front half. Crease on dashed lines.

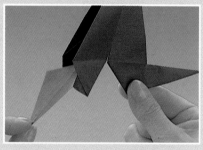

2. Open left portion and fold down on crease.

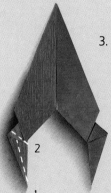

3. Repeat on right side. Crease on dashed lines 1 and 2.

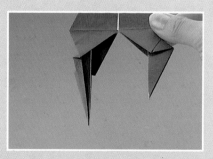

4. On crease 1 fold forward and crease on 2 inside.

5. Repeat on right side. Turn form over and repeat procedure. On dashed line . . .

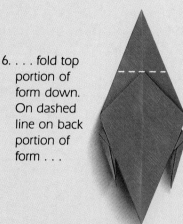

6. . . . fold top portion of form down. On dashed line on back portion of form . . .

7. . . . fold point back. Crease both left and right legs on dashed lines.

8. Open left portion and fold upwards to the left.

9. Repeat on right side, reversing instructions.

13. . . . crease outer edge. Open as shown and fold corners inside. Turn form over . . .

17. Open crease again and fold down.

10. Fold form in half on midline and turn as shown. On dashed line . . .

14. . . . and repeat procedures. Turn form over again.

18. Press fold down.

11. . . . crease to give tail its direction. Open crease and fold down.

15. Open tail and pull upwards on crease 2 of Step 12—as shown.

19. Insert back half into front half and glue together.

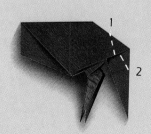

12. Fold on dashed lines. On dashed line 1 . . .

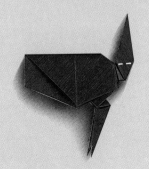

16. Fold form together. Crease tail on dashed line.

20. Set your horse on his feet.

Rider

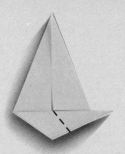

3. Flatten. Crease on dashed line.

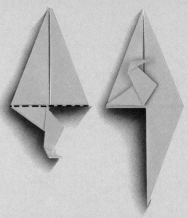

7. Fold left portion up at dashed line and fold right upper triangle back down.

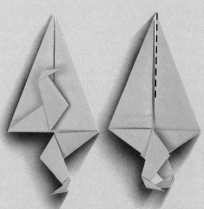

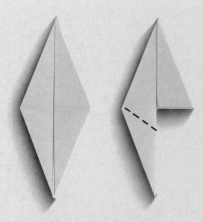

1. Start with Basic Form VII (page 40), the "split" side pointing down. Fold lower right point up at midline to the front. Crease on dashed line.

5. Crease on dashed line.

8. Repeat Steps 2–7 with the right portion, in reverse. Fold down again that portion that was folded up in Step 7. Cut front point down the midline as shown.

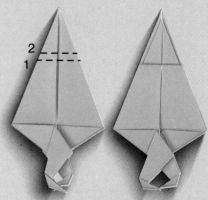

2. Open fold of left portion and bend right at crease.

6. Open that portion and bend to the right on the crease.

9. Turn form over. Fold point down to the inside at dashed line 1 and back up again on line 2.

4. Open that portion and bend down on the crease.

44

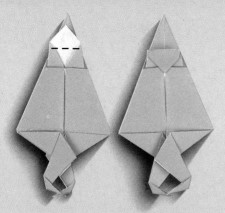

10. Open the just-created triangle, fold down on dashed line, and flatten creases.

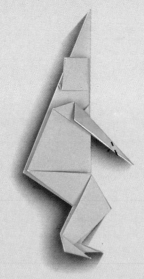

13. . . . and fold arm in half with crease at top. Crease arm on dashed line.

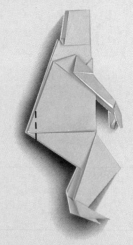

16. Turn form over and repeat Steps 11–15. Fold inward at dashed line.

11. Fold form in half at the midline with folds inside. On dashed line . . .

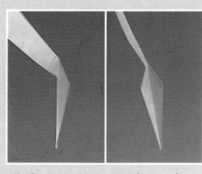

14. Open up lower portion to the crease.

17. Pull head slightly to the right.

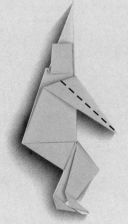

12. . . . fold top triangle down. Crease on dashed line . . .

15. Pull that portion a little to the left, fold tip of fingers inside.

18. Dress your rider with a hat (page 63) and let him mount his horse.

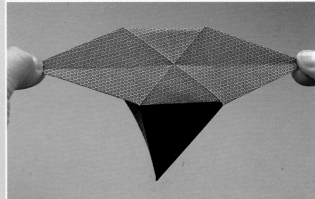

3. . . . the paper, by unfolding itself, is flat.

Dragon

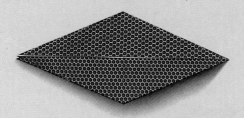

1. Start with Basic Form VII (page 40), "split" side pointing to the right. Pull both left points . . .

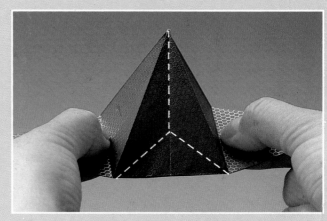

4. Turn form over. On dashed lines press both points that are almost upright . . .

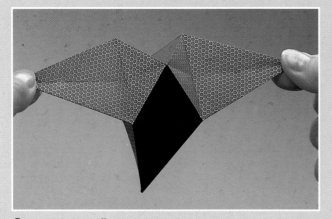

2. . . . apart, until . . .

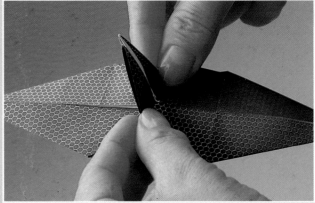

5. . . . together in the middle until they are lying flat on the surface . . .

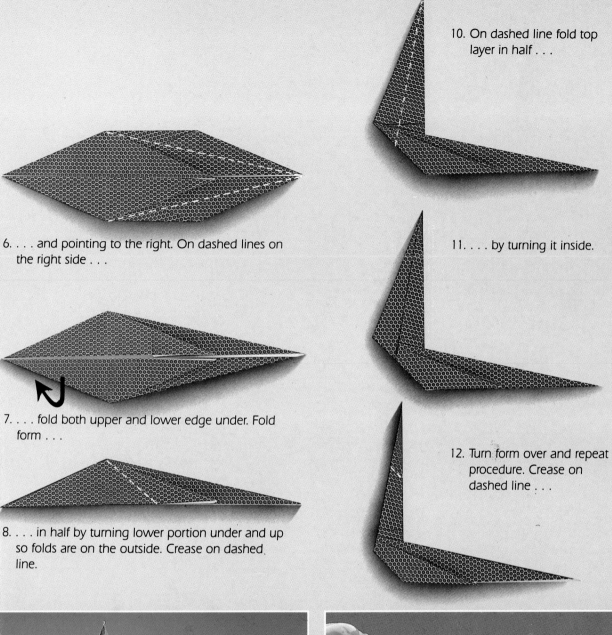

6. . . . and pointing to the right. On dashed lines on the right side . . .

7. . . . fold both upper and lower edge under. Fold form . . .

8. . . . in half by turning lower portion under and up so folds are on the outside. Crease on dashed line.

10. On dashed line fold top layer in half . . .

11. . . . by turning it inside.

12. Turn form over and repeat procedure. Crease on dashed line . . .

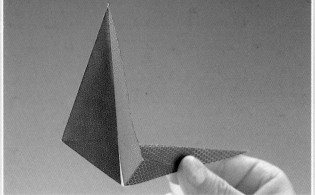

9. Open left portion of form and fold point up and inside on crease.

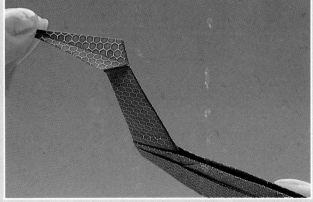

13. . . . open that portion and fold down on crease.

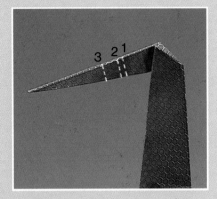

14. Crease on dashed lines 1, 2, and 3.

17. . . . fold up again on crease 3.

20. Fold small point in half on dashed line . . .

15. Fold up on crease 1.

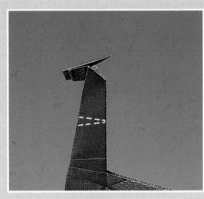

18. Crease on dashed lines . . .

21. . . . and down. Turn form over and repeat. Crease on dashed line . . .

16. Fold down on crease 2, and . . .

19. . . . and fold lower crease inside and upper crease out again.

22. . . . open that portion and fold up.

48

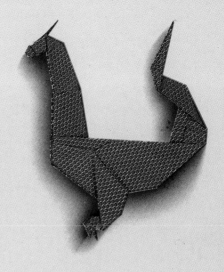

23. Crease on dashed lines.

26. Crease on dashed lines.

29. Turn dragon over and repeat procedure.

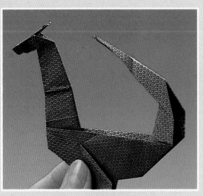

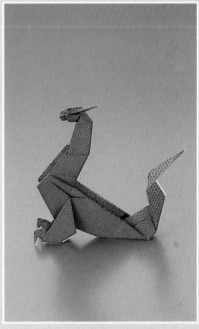

24. Open fold and turn lower crease left . . .

27. Turn point on upper crease left . . .

30. Your dragon is ready for action.

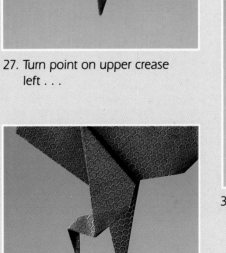

25. . . . and upper crease up.

28. . . . and on lower crease down.

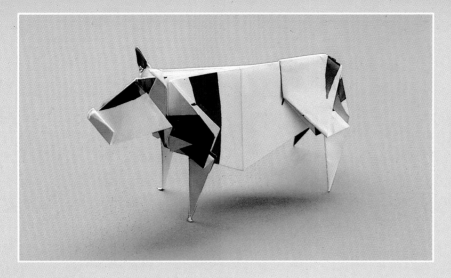

Cow

1. You will need two pieces of paper, both square in shape, one of which should be ¼ the size of the other.

3. Turn form over and crease sharply on dashed lines.

6. Crease on dashed line and fold the right and left upper edges so that they meet at the vertical midline.

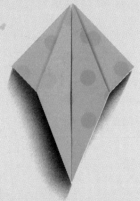

2. Fold the larger of the two pieces according to instructions for Basic Form VII (page 40) up to Step 8 and position as shown.

4. Pull left top portion up . . .

7. Unfold last folds, open form and fold both edges on the creases just established, so that they will meet at the midline.

50

8. Fold small triangle up. Fold small right wing to . . .

11. . . . fold both top points on the left side to the right. Crease on dashed lines 1 and 2.

15. Turn small point outside at the crease . . .

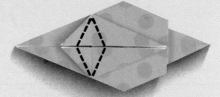

9. . . . the left. Repeat Steps 4–8 on right portion of form. Turn form over.

12. Fold right point back and underneath on crease 1, and on 2 out again. On top triangles make creases as shown.

16. . . . as the form is folded together again.

13. Fold form together by turning back top portion on midline.

17. Turn right middle point (see Step 13) inside at the crease.

10. Hold as shown, with open portion pointing left. On dashed line . . .

14. Open top wing upwards.

18. Flatten form. On dashed line . . .

19. . . . fold edge a little forward.

20. Turn form over and repeat Steps 13–19. Crease on dashed lines 1 and 2. On line 1 . . .

21. . . . fold right point up . . .

22. . . . and on 2 fold inside.

23. Flatten folds. On dashed lines . . .

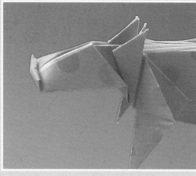

24. . . . roll left point upwards.

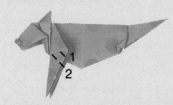

25. Fold form together. Crease on dashed lines 1 and 2.

26. Fold front leg on crease 1 inside . . .

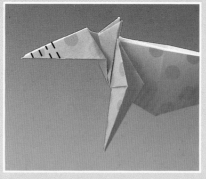

27. . . . and on 2 outside.

28. Press folds down. On dashed line . . .

29. . . . fold edge inside.

30. Turn form over and repeat Steps 25–29.

52

31. Hindlegs: use the small piece of paper. Crease on dashed line.

35. Glue this form around the back portion of the cow as shown.

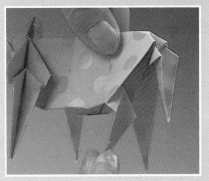

39. . . . and 3 outside again.

32. Fold left and right edges so that they meet on the diagonal line.

36. Crease on dashed lines 1, 2, and 3.

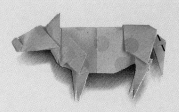

40. Turn form over and repeat procedure. On dashed line . . .

33. Repeat for upper and lower edges.

37. Open right point and fold on crease 1 to the inside.

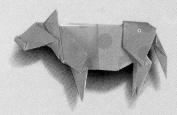

41. . . . fold tail down as shown.

34. Fold form in half at the diagonal line, with the previous folds to the inside.

38. Open hindleg and fold crease 2 inside . . .

42. Now shape the horns.

53

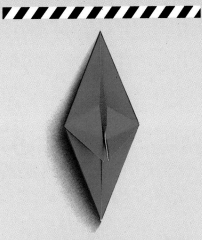

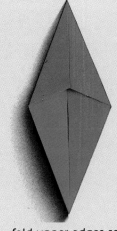

BASIC FORM VIII

3. . . . fold upper edges so that they meet at the vertical midline.

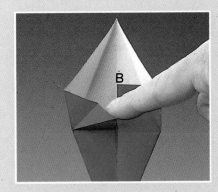

6. . . . up . . .

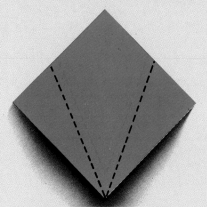

1. A square piece of paper is creased twice diagonally. On dashed lines fold both lower edges . . .

4. Fold form together at the horizontal midline.

7. . . . then pull down and flatten.

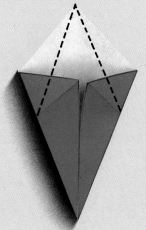

2. . . . so that they meet at the midline (white side of paper inside). On dashed lines . . .

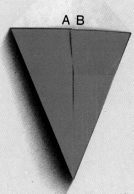

5. Unfold Steps 3 and 4. Lift corner A . . .

8. Repeat with corner B. Flatten folds. This is Basic Form VIII.

Chick

1. Start with Basic Form VIII, the points of the small wings pointing to the right.

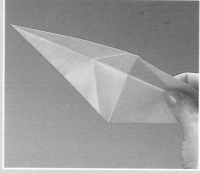

3. . . . crease, then open form from below.

6. Open upper point and fold to the left.

2. Fold form in half, with open edges on top. On dashed line . . .

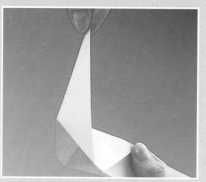

4. Now open left portion a little and fold up and to the right. Flatten folds.

7. Crease on dashed lines 1 and 2.

56

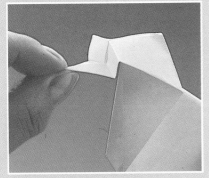

8. Fold crease 1 to the inside, and 2 to the outside again.

12. . . . and fold crease 1 to the left . . .

15. On dashed line . . .

9. Fold small wing to the left . . .

13. . . . 2 to the right . . .

16. . . . fold lower right edge inside. Turn form over and repeat.

10. . . . and on dashed line to the right again. Turn form over and repeat Steps 9 and 10. These are the wings.

11. Crease on dashed lines 1, 2, and 3 . . .

14. . . . 3 to the left again. This is the foot.

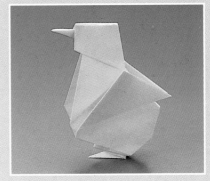

17. This is the little chick.

5. Open fold and fold down on crease 1 . . .

6. . . . up on 2 . . .

Rooter

1. Start with Basic Form VIII (page 55), with the point of the small wing pointing to the right.

3. . . . fold right point upwards at the crease.

7. . . . on 3 down again . . .

2. Fold form in half with the folds outside. On dashed line . . .

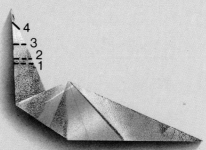

4
3
2
1

4. Crease top portion of form on dashed lines 1, 2, 3 and 4.

8. . . . and on 4, pull to the left.

58

9. On dashed line . . .

13. Open right portion . . .

17. . . . and down on 2.

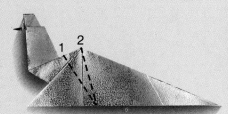

10. . . . fold small wings left. Crease on dashed lines 1 and 2.

14. . . . and fold inside on the crease.

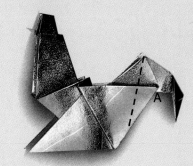

18. On dashed line . . .

11. Fold 1 to the left, and 2 to the right again.

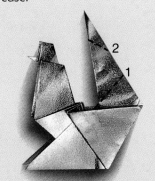

15. Crease on dashed lines 1 and 2.

19. . . . fold corner A to the left. Turn form over and repeat procedure.

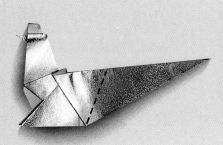

12. Crease on dashed line.

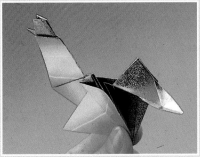

16. Open that portion and fold crease 1 inside to the right . . .

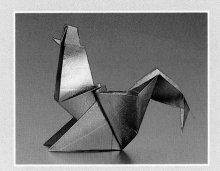

20. This is your rooster.

7. On dashed lines . . .

Dog

1. Start with Basic Form VIII (page 55), small triangle pointing right. Fold left point back on vertical midline.

4. . . . and down along line 2. Lift right top portion straight up, and fold it together . . .

8. . . . fold both upper and lower right edges so that they meet at the horizontal midline. Fold form together at the midline, folds inside.

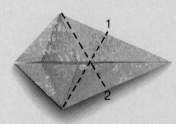

2. Fold small point to the left. On dashed lines crease . . .

5. . . . on its horizontal midline until it meets the point of the crease. Flatten its base . . .

9. Crease on dashed lines 1 and 2.

3. . . . by folding the top right portion up along line 1 . . .

6. . . . and fold new triangle down. Turn form over.

10. Fold top point on crease 2 to the right, and on 1 to the left.

11. Crease on dashed lines 1, 2, and 3.

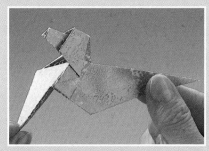

15. Fold both left points down on the crease, while at the same time folding form together again.

19. Open right portion of form and fold up on crease 1.

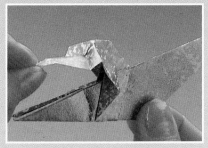

12. Fold top point down on crease 1 to the inside, and on 2 out again.

16. Flatten and crease on dashed line.

20. On crease 2 fold the tip of the forelegs inside.

13. On crease 3 fold inside again.

17. Fold right point down and to the inside.

21. Crease small lower corner on dashed line . . .

14. Open form from the bottom and crease on dashed lines.

18. Crease on dashed lines 1 and 2.

22. . . . and fold inside on both sides.

61

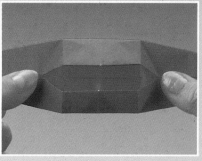

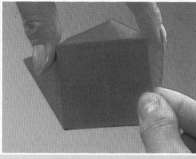

6. Fold upper and lower edges of both sides of form towards the horizontal midline.

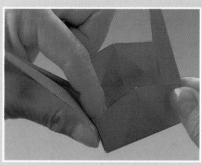

7. Turn form over and shape bottom along creases into a square.

Basket

1. Begin with Basic Form VIII (page 55), the tips of the small wing pointing to the right. Crease on dashed lines.

3. . . . and flatten it down. Fold the lower tip of the shape just created on the dashed line, under and to the inside.

4. On dashed line on the left tip . . .

8. Push corners together along the established creases.

2. Lift upper small triangular form up at the tip, open it . . .

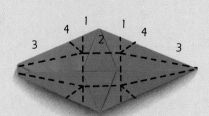

4   1   1   4
3   2   3

5. . . . fold to the right. Repeat Steps 2–4 with the lower triangular form. Crease on dashed lines in order given.

9. Pull handles up and slide them into each other.

SHAPES MADE OUT OF DIFFERENT FORMS

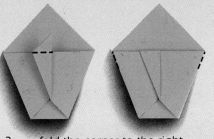

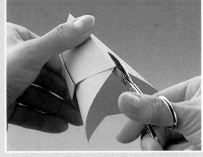

3. . . . fold the corner to the right. On dashed line fold tip down and to the inside. On dashed line on each side . . .

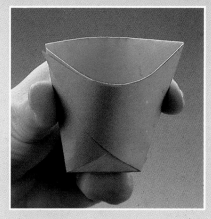

Cup

Cowboy Hat

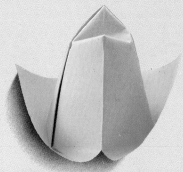

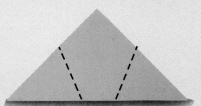

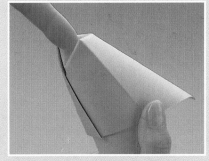

4. . . . cut and open form slowly. Insert fingers between top two triangles . . .

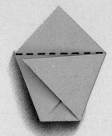

1. Begin on Step 2 of Cowboy Hat. On dashed line . . .

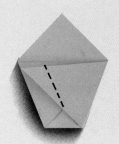

1. Fold a square piece of paper diagonally. On dashed lines first fold the left corner to the right . . .

5. . . . and push bottom inside.

2. . . . tuck upper top corner into top triangle.

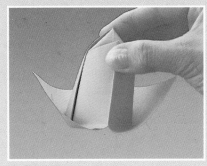

2. . . . then the right corner to the left as shown. On dashed line . . .

6. Fold both corners up to shape hat.

3. Tuck other triangle inside. To open form: push in from both sides.

63

Plane

1. Take a square piece of paper . . .

2. . . . and fold diagonally. On dashed line . . .

3. . . . fold top lower corner up. On dashed line 1 . . .

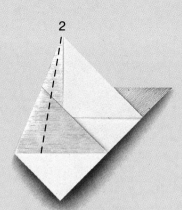

4. . . . fold left portion of form towards the right edge. On dashed line 2 . . .

7. . . . fold portion back towards the right. Fold upper point down on the lower dashed line . . .

10. Open right point and fold inside on crease.

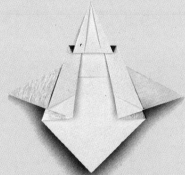

5. . . . fold that portion back towards left. On dashed line 3 . . .

8. . . . and up again on the top line.

11. Crease on dashed line.

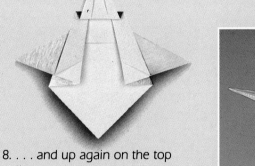

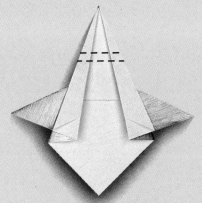

6. . . . fold right portion of form towards the left edge. On dashed line 4 . . .

9. Fold form together in the middle, folds inside, and hold horizontally. Crease on dashed line.

12. Hold plane below that crease and fold upper part down at the crease to create the wings.

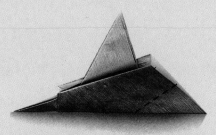

13. Your plane is ready for take-off!

65

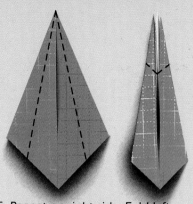

5. Repeat on right side. Fold left and right edges back on dashed lines (left). Crease on dashed lines (right).

Lady

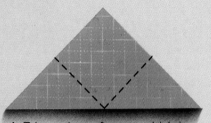

1. Take a piece of paper which is a right-angled triangle (half of a square). On dashed lines . . .

3. Open left half of form and . . .

6. Open left top point and fold to the left on crease.

2. . . . fold left and right corners up to meet at the top corner. Crease on dashed lines.

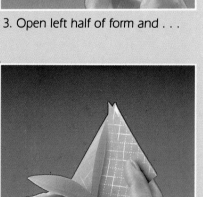

4. . . . fold the left outer portion inside at the crease. Fold new triangle upwards.

7. Repeat on right side. These are the arms. Fold lower corner up as shown.

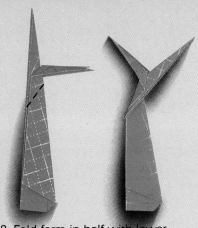

8. Fold form in half with lower folded-up corner inside. Crease on dashed line.

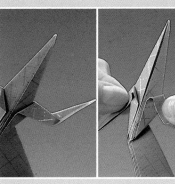

11. Open arm and bend up on crease. Pull both shoulders down.

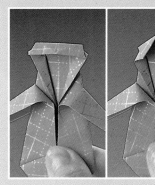

14. . . . down again on line 2. Press left and right corners forward.

9. Hold form below crease, open up upper portion and flatten.

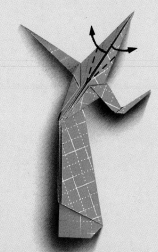

12. Open upper portion and fold . . .

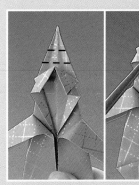

15. Now fold the point that is in the back up and over on lower dashed line, and tuck point under on upper line.

10. Crease right arm on dashed line.

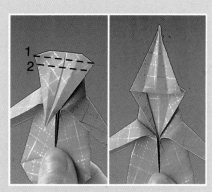

13. . . . down on dashed lines. Fold this portion up on dashed line 1, and . . .

16. On dashed line fold the top portion of the skirt up to the right. Give the lady a face and she will be ready to go.

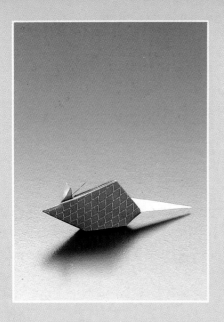

4. On dashed lines fold upper and lower edges . . .

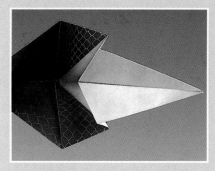

8. Turn form over, open up and fold the long edges of the diamond . . .

Mouse

1. Take a piece of paper which is a right-angled triangle. Crease on dashed line 1, fold top point down on 2, and fold bottom point up on 3 so that they meet at crease 1.

2
1
3

5. . . . so that they will meet on the reverse side at the horizontal midline.

6. Fold form in half along the midline. On dashed line 1 fold right point inside . . .

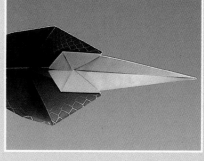

9. . . . together on the midline.

2. Fold at dashed lines towards the left.

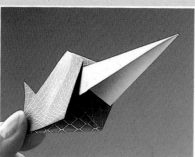

3. On dashed lines fold up- per and lower corners on the right so that they meet at the horizontal midline.

7. . . . and on dashed line 2 fold outside.

10. Fold form together again. Next: on dashed line fold both lower corners . . .

11. . . . inside. This is the mouse.

68

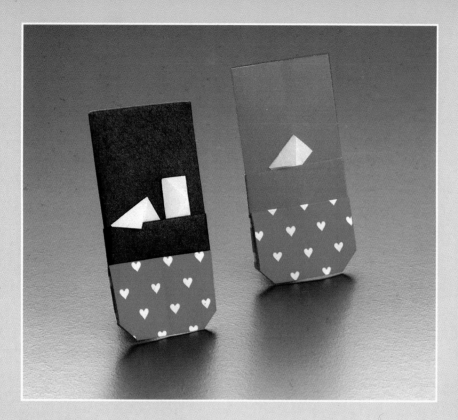

3. . . . fold both corners.

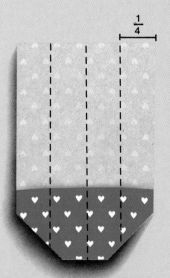

4. Open left wing and fold corner inside.

Letter Holder

1. You will need a rectangular piece of paper that, if folded in half, represents two equal squares.

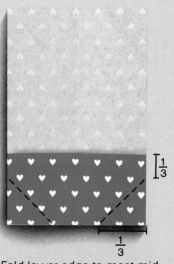

2. Fold lower edge to meet mid-line (white side of paper inside). On dashed lines . . .

$\frac{1}{3}$

$\frac{1}{3}$

$\frac{1}{4}$

5. Repeat on right side. Crease sharply on dashed lines.

6. Open the pocket shape again and fold . . .

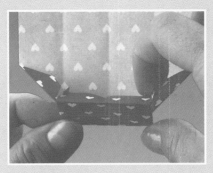

9. . . . inside.

12. . . . and on 2 up again. Turn form over and fold both edges on dashed lines . . .

7. . . . left top corner inside.

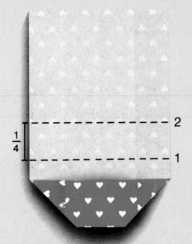

$\frac{1}{4}$

2

1

10. Fold upper portion of form on dashed line 1 . . .

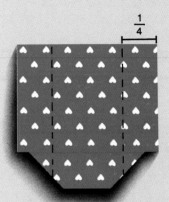

$\frac{1}{4}$

13. . . . so that they meet on the vertical midline.

8. Repeat on right side. Turn upper middle edge of pocket . . .

11. . . . back . . .

14. Turn form over. Hang on the wall as a message holder!

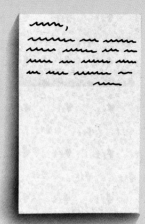

2. . . . and unfold paper. The upper portion above the dashed line is for your note. If the space is too small and you need more room, use a piece of paper that is longer above the dashed line.

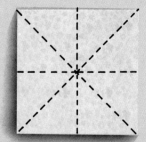

3. When you are finished with your letter fold that part into accordion folds.

Folded Letter

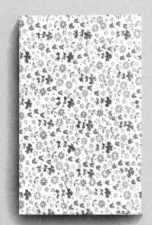

You need a rectangular piece of paper that, if folded in half, represents two equal squares.

1. Fold lower right edge up along the left long edge. Crease on dashed line . . .

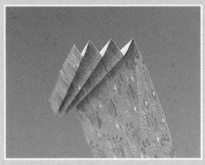

4. The lower portion must be a square. Fold this portion as follows: crease on dashed lines . . .

72

5. . . . and fold paper together from the bottom up to the midline.

9. Lift right top wing up.

13. Open upper point . . .

6. Lift the left half of the form up.

10. Open fold and flatten.

14. . . . pull it down to the lower point and flatten.

7. Open fold and flatten.

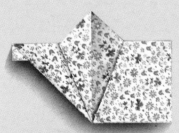

11. Fold left and right upper edges of this portion down to meet on midline.

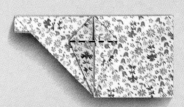

15. Fold lower point up on dashed line.

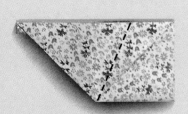

8. Crease on dashed line.

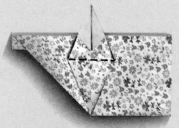

12. Crease form on dashed line and unfold.

16. You now have a diamond shape. Fold right half of this shape . . .

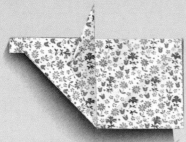

17. . . . to the left.

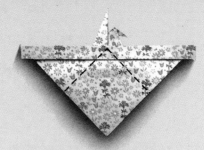

21. Fold upper left and right corners on dashed lines . . .

Baby Bird

18. Repeat Steps 6–15 with the right half of the form. Fold left wing of diamond to the right. On dashed line . . .

22. . . . down to meet at lower point. On the points marked "X" pull a ribbon through.

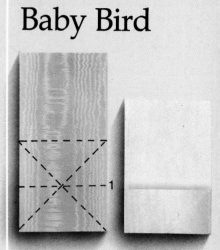

1. You need a rectangular piece of paper whose halves must be two equal squares. Crease on dashed lines. Fold up on crease 1.

19. . . . crease and fold down and back.

20. Turn form over.

23. Turn letter over. Tie the ribbon.

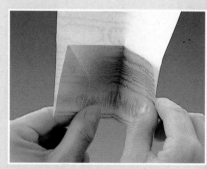

2. Lift left half of paper up . . .

3. . . . open fold and flatten.

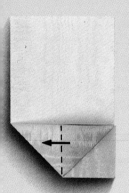

4. Fold right triangle on dashed line . . .

5. . . . to the left.

6. Repeat Steps 2–5, reversed, with the right portion. On dashed lines . . .

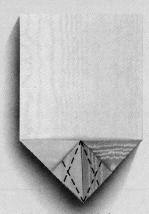

7. . . . fold right and left upper corners of triangle down to the bottom corner. Fold along dashed lines.

8. With the two center points down on the midline, fold and push the two opposite corners together along the vertical midline. This is the bird's beak.

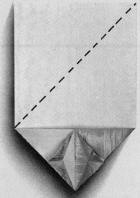

9. Fold upper portion of paper diagonally.

10. Turn form as shown. On dashed lines . . .

11. . . . fold upper and lower edges to the back. On dashed line 1 . . .

12. . . . fold back again. On line 2 . . .

13. . . . fold left portion back and up to form the tail. Glue or paint eyes on and your baby bird is ready.

75

2. . . . fold right half over to the left, open fold again.

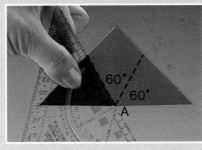

3. Position protractor on center point and mark your required dashed lines at 60° and 120° angles.

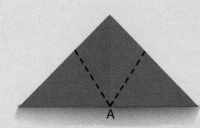

4. Crease triangle on dashed lines.

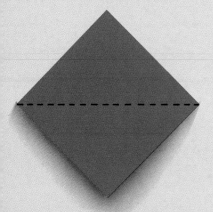

For the snowflakes and marguerites you need pieces of paper in the shape of a hexagon. To create these you will need the following:

—a square piece of paper
—a protractor
—a pair of scissors.

HEXAGON

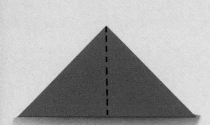

1. Fold a square piece of paper diagonally. On dashed line . . .

5. Fold right portion to the left . . .

6. . . . and left portion to the right. Flatten folds sharply.

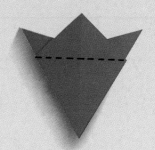

7. Turn form over and . . .

8. . . . cut along dashed line.

9. Open all folds. This is your hexagon shape.

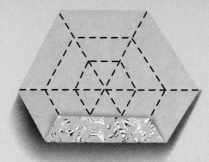

4. Fold lower edge "I" on the bottom crease up by ⅓.

8. Proceed around the hexagon in like manner. Turn paper over.

Snowflakes

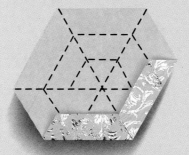

5. Do likewise with edge "II."

1. Prepare paper according to instructions on page 77 up to Step 8, the closed tip pointing down. On dashed lines . . .

2. . . . crease the triangle.

3. Open all folds.

6. Open last two folds. Pull out lower right corner.

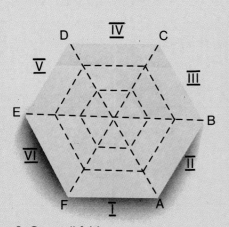

7. Now fold edge "II" and then edge "I" down again, while the corner remains outside.

9. Fold edge "1" on middle creased line (see Step 3) . . .

10. . . . up to the midline.

11. Fold edge "2" likewise, but . . .

2. . . . at the same time as you pull down point "F," fold point to the left.

16. . . . meet in the middle.

20. Open fold and flatten it.

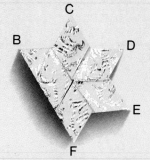

3. Repeat around form with remaining edges.

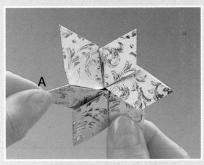

17. The fold that has been pulled out is folded to the left.

21. Repeat with remaining points. This is the first snowflake.

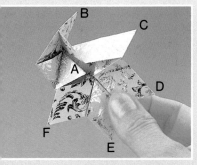

4. Open last fold and pull out point "A" . . .

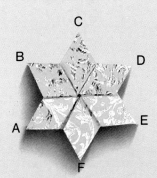

18. Your form now has six points.

22. Turn form over. This is the second snowflake.

23. If you fold the side edges of each point back on the dashed lines . . .

5. . . . so that the center points of edges 5 and 6 . . .

19. Pull a point up vertically.

24. . . . you have the third snowflake.

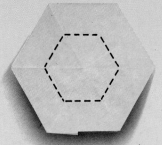

2. Crease yellow paper and glue it in the center so that all creases match.

5. On dashed lines in the center . . .

Marguerite

You need two pieces of paper in hexagon shape:

—one white for the petals
—one yellow for the center.

The white paper must be exactly three times the size of the yellow paper.

3. Now fold up to Step 21 on page 79.

6. . . . fold all points out and up.

1. Fold white paper up to Step 9 of the Snowflake on page 78.

4. On dashed lines fold all corners under.

7. Fasten a stem onto the back.

Index